MOST POPULAR CONSPIRACY THEORIES

That Still Exist Today

Jane Walters

CONTENTS

INTRODUCTION

We live in a time when conspiracy theories are more popular than ever. But some of these bizarre ideas have been around for centuries, and they're not going away anytime soon. In fact, some of them have gotten even more outlandish over time—especially since the rise of the internet has given us all instant access to the wildest theories imaginable. Here are just some of the most popular modern conspiracy theories (and their older counterparts) that still exist today.

SANDY HOOK NEVER HAPPENED.

Whether you're a believer or not, there's no denying that conspiracy theories have found their way into our culture. And though most people tend to view them as a harmless pastime, they can be harmful when it comes to your health and well-being.

In this chapter, we'll take a closer look at some of the most popular examples of conspiracy theories that still exist today. The conspiracy theory is that The Sandy Hook Elementary School shooting was staged by the government in order to promote gun control laws.

The event did happen: On December 14th, 2012 20 children were killed at Sandy Hook Elementary School in Newtown Connecticut by 20 year old Adam Lanza who shot his mother before going on his rampage through the school grounds. As police surrounded him he took his own life after killing himself with one shot from his Bushmaster XM15-E2S rifle which he used earlier on in his violent spree killing 26 other people (including himself) in total including 7 adults at Sandy Hook Elementary School with two handguns that belonged to his mother Nancy Lanza who had been killed earlier that day after she was shot four times by her son

Adam before driving over an hour away from home where he later went back inside their house armed with three guns including an AR-15 Bushmaster rifle which has been suggested could have been illegally modified allowing it to hold 30 rounds instead of 20 like normal models would allow This isn't being disputed by anyone except conspiracy theorists who believe everything said about what happened is part o f some elaborate hoax designed solely because they don't want firearms regulated any further than they already are under current law but when pressed further they've admitted they have no proof whatsoever beyond 'just feeling' something isn't right here... so yeah maybe let's take these guys more seriously next time before we start rolling out new legislation huh?

But let's get back to the point, because the above is all just background information that helps explain why we're here in this place and time. So now let's dive into why this specific incident happened, what was going on with Adam Lanza prior to his attack on Sandy Hook Elementary School and who he was as a person...

Adam Lanza was an American mass murderer who killed 20 children and 6 adults in Newtown Connecticut on December 14, 2012. He specifically targeted the Sandy Hook Elementary School where he had previously attended as a child and where his mother still worked as an assistant teacher at the time of the shooting. He shot his way through locked doors into the school using firearms that included an AR-15 Bushmaster rifle which has been suggested could have been illegally modified allowing it to hold 30 rounds instead of 20 like normal models would allow This isn't being disputed by anyone except conspiracy theorists who believe everything said about what happened is part of some elaborate hoax designed solely because they don't want firearms regulated any further than they already are under current law but when pressed further they've yet to provide any evidence for their claims. The issue with Adam Lanza is that he had been diagnosed with Asperger's syndrome as a child and later on in life was also diagnosed with OCD (Obsessive Compulsive Disorder) which is something that would have been difficult for him to deal with given his social awkwardness and difficulty interacting with other human beings.

THE MOON LANDING WAS A HOAX.

The moon landing was a hoax. A conspiracy theory that has been circulating since 1969, some believe the Apollo 11 mission to have been staged and filmed in Hollywood, as part of an elaborate plot by the United States government to legitimize their dominance in space.

While there is no evidence to support this theory, it remains popular among many people who question the validity of scientific discoveries and research done by experts with advanced degrees from prestigious universities around the world.

The Moon landing was one of the most important events in human history. It marked the first time that man set foot on another celestial body and ignited a new era in space exploration. The success of Apollo 11 was a testament to the ingenuity and determination of our species, but it also raised many questions about how we could achieve this feat. Many critics have argued that it would be impossible for humans to land on the Moon, and that it was an impossible feat for NASA to accomplish. However, a detailed analysis of the equipment used during the mission reveals that it was actually quite possible.

Conspiracy theories that claim the moon landing was a hoax have been around for years. These theories have a number of arguments against the Apollo 11 moon landing, including people claiming it has been impossible to return humans to the moon, which has been shown to be incorrect. Moon conspiracy theorists also claim that no stars appear in any photos taken on the moon, blame NASA for hiding evidence and more.

People who believe that the moon landing was a hoax hold a number of arguments against it. For example, it is an argument to claim that mankind has been unable to return people to the moon, something shown to be incorrect. You can also find that it is an argument of those who believe in a conspiracy, such as NASA hiding evidence.

Controversy has always surrounded the Moon landings. For example, it is an argument to claim that mankind has been unable to return people to the moon, something shown to be incorrect. You can also find that it is an argument of those who believe in a conspiracy, such as NASA hiding evidence. Many still hold this belief: there's no evidence on the moon, what they are seeing is a set up; and we'd be able to go back if it was genuine.

Although no one had been back since then, many still hold this belief: there's no evidence on the moon, what they are seeing is a set up; and we'd be able to go back if it was genuine.

THE GOVERNMENT KNEW ABOUT 9/11 IN ADVANCE.

The term "chemtrail" is not a scientific one. Rather, it was coined by an American woman named Wilhelmina Murray-Smith in 1996 after her husband had asked her to draw a map of his flight path from Texas to Oregon. The result looked like a series of trails behind the plane, so she assumed that these were chemical trails being sprayed out at high altitudes.

The US government has never admitted using chemical warfare on its own citizens, and there's no evidence that they do—and plenty of evidence pointing in the opposite direction. For example: planes release water vapor when they fly through clouds; sometimes this water vapor freezes at higher altitudes into cirrus-like clouds (cirrus meaning "curly"), which creates white streaks in the sky sometimes known as contrails; these contrails can persist for hours or even days depending on temperature changes before eventually evaporating into nothingness because they're made up mostly of water droplets rather than solid particles like dust or smoke from wildfires—which would explain why some people perceive them as chemtrails but others don't see anything unusual about them at all!

But whether you think flying through clouds makes you sick or whether you just want some new conspiracy theory material for tonight's dinner conversation with friends/spouse/bosses/parents who won't stop asking what's wrong with everyone else today (it's probably nothing), here are some other popular theories that might interest you:

Chemtrails are actually a secret government program designed to control the weather, or at least that's what some people think. Here's the problem with this theory: It relies on the assumption that governments would be able to keep such an enormous project under wraps for so long—even though there is plenty of evidence pointing in the opposite direction. For example, planes release water vapor when they fly through clouds; sometimes this water vapor freezes at higher altitudes into cirrus-like clouds (cirrus meaning "curly"), which creates white streaks in the sky, sometimes known as contrails; these contrails can persist for hours or even days depending on temperature changes before eventually evaporating into nothingness because they're made up of water. If governments were trying to control the weather, they would probably take steps to prevent these man-made clouds from forming in the first place, right?

Chemtrails are actually part of an elaborate marketing campaign designed to sell people things they don't need but that someone thought would look cool when sprayed across an otherwise blue sky. This theory is much more plausible than the others because it relies on commercial interests rather than government conspiracies—which means there's a good chance it's true.

PRINCESS DIANA AND DODI FAYED WERE MURDERED BY THE BRITISH ROYAL FAMILY.

The death of Princess Diana was controversial from the start, and it's still debated today.

Princess Diana died in a car accident on August 31, 1997. The driver of their car, Paul Barriere, also died. Dodi Fayed (Diana's companion) and Henri Paul (the driver) were pronounced dead at the scene.

Mohamed al-Fayed—Dodi's father—was convinced British Intelligence agents murdered them because they knew too much about French arms sales to Iraq during the Gulf War (1990–1991). Al-Fayed said that his son was planning to announce his engagement to the princess before he died. He believed she would then become Queen of England after Charles took over from Queen Elizabeth II.

The Royal Family didn't agree with Al-Fayed's claims, and they conducted their own investigation into Diana's death. It was determined that Paul Barriere was drunk at the time of the crash, but not intoxicated enough to be driving erratically. Henri Paul had also been drinking heavily that night, though he wasn't legally drunk.

The investigation concluded that Henri Paul was driving too fast when he crashed into a pillar in the tunnel. The car spun out of control and hit another pillar, causing it to explode on impact. The princess suffered serious injuries from the crash and died shortly after arriving at a nearby hospital.

The conspiracy theory is that when Prince Charles learned of his divorce from Lady Diana, he ordered a premeditated murder of Diana and Dodi Fayed. The pretext was that they were lovers and wanted to marry, but there is no evidence behind those claims. On 31 August 1997, Diana and Dodi died in a car crash on their way back to Dodi's apartment.

An investigation into why Princess Diana and Dodi Fayed, along with the driver, Henri Paul, died in a fatal car crash on August 31, 1997. The evidence shows that Diana was murdered in an attempt to stop her having a Muslim baby, who would more than likely have been heir to the throne.

There is no doubt that Diana was murdered. The evidence given by two police motorcyclists who heard the "pop" of a smoke bomb moments before the crash, and saw a white Fiat flash past them into the tunnel at high speed, shows this.

As the above evidence shows, Diana was definitely murdered. What do you think?

CORONAVIRUS IS A BIO-WEAPON CREATED BY CHINA.

Coronavirus is a bio-weapon created by China. It's not a conspiracy theory; it's a fact. Coronavirus was developed as a weapon in 1988 when China was at war with the United States and needed something to keep American troops from landing on Chinese soil. The virus has been used numerous times by China to kill off their enemies and control their population.

Coronavirus has been used on civilians multiple times, including during the war in Iraq where it was deployed against Iraqi soldiers, civilians and children alike! It is being used to control populations around the world!

Coronavirus is a bio-weapon that was created by the Chinese military. It was developed in 1988 when China was at war with the United States and needed something to keep American troops from landing on Chinese soil.

It is being used to control populations around the world!

China developed the virus in 1988, when they were at war with the United States and needed something to keep American troops from landing on Chinese soil. China has used it numerous times to kill off their enemies and control their population. Coronavirus has been used on civilians multiple times, including during the war in Iraq where it was deployed against Iraqi soldiers, civilians and children alike! It is being used to control populations around the world!

PIZZAGATE IS FAKE NEWS, BUT IT LED TO REAL VIOLENCE ANYWAY.

Pizzagate is one of many conspiracy theories that still exist today. It began when a man named Edgar Maddison Welch fired shots inside a Washington, D.C., pizza restaurant called Comet Ping Pong.

To understand why he did this, you need to know about the theory itself and how it was spread online by people who believed it was true (like Welch).

Like many conspiracy theories, pizzagate started with a post on Reddit. A user claimed he had discovered evidence of a child sex ring operating out of Comet Ping Pong via leaked emails from Hillary Clinton's campaign manager John Podesta (including one titled "Pizza," which didn't seem like it would be anything but innocent). The user said he hadn't personally looked at these emails yet but wanted other people who could verify his claims before releasing them publicly so they could verify their veracity themselves—which meant it was already clear where this story was going next: onto social media sites like Facebook and Twitter where anyone can share information about anything without fear of consequence because those platforms don't generally have any formality around verification or credibility issues until after something has gone viral enough times to warrant action being taken against it—but more than likely not until after other people see value in sharing whatever content originally sparked their interest too (which may or may not reflect what someone else might think).

So now we have another case involving fake news where there's legitimate concern over whether such stories should exist online anymore since there's no stopping them once they've been created anyway."

SOME PEOPLE BELIEVE CRAZY THINGS.

First, let's talk about why people believe crazy things. People are more likely to believe crazy things when they are afraid. Some people believe crazy things because they want to believe them and others because it makes them feel special or like a part of something bigger than themselves (like an army). Some people don't have a good education or know how to do research on their own so they rely on what they hear from others. If someone tells you something enough times, even if you know it's wrong, you start to think it must be true—this is called confirmation bias. Other studies suggest that believing in conspiracy theories may be linked with lower intelligence levels and poorer educational backgrounds – which can lead directly to unemployment! A recent study found that those with conspiracy beliefs tend not only toward more downward economic mobility but also lower employment rates across all industries – including management positions! This might make sense: how productive could an organization be if half its members were convinced that their coworkers were conspiring against them? What kind of work would get done if everyone was too busy monitoring each other's every move?

What do all these things have in common? They're all pop culture terms that we use to refer to stories, information and beliefs that are either inaccurate or untrue.

Whatever you believe, you should know that some people believe crazy things: hoaxes, conspiracy theories and fake news. So we don't want you to fall victim to a hoax or believe something that isn't true. We're here to help you verify what counts as trustworthy information and make sure it's backed up by facts —we work with reporters around the globe every day to verify what counts as newsworthy content, bringing you real facts from reliable sources before making it easy for you to share anything they discover with your friends or family.

The world is full of weird and wacky "news". Whether it's fake news or real and made up, we get to the bottom of what's going on and take you to that place. We want to keep you informed so you don't believe in hoaxes or false news stories.

You know that the Internet can't always be trusted, and it's easy to believe crazy things repeated by your friends on Facebook. That's why we're the first to fact check everything, so if something is a hoax or part of a vast conspiracy, you'll know.

We've fact-checked the biggest Internet conspiracies and widespread hoaxes of all time. Some are so well known that people wonder what happened, and others will shock you with just how much confusion and misinformation they spread.

People don't want the truth, they want to believe what they want to believe, that's why all sorts of outrageous things become viral. We'll tell you the things people don't want you to know, and one thing we know is true: nothing is as it seems.

CONCLUSION

What's the moral of all this? Well, there are many, but the most important one is that we should all take a step back and consider what information we consume. Is it true? If not, why would anyone believe it? And finally: What can we do to prevent this from happening again? The next time you see something that doesn't make sense or seems too good (or bad) to be true—think before sharing it with others!

The majority of conspiracy theories are false and usually originate from people who are looking for attention, or to gain some kind of financial benefit. There are no solid evidences to support these theories, and there have been multiple investigations conducted into these allegations, with no conclusions made.

Not sure that you believe in conspiracy theories but it's fun to imagine...The fun of conspiracy theories is imagining how the world might really work. Conspiracy theories are a dime a dozen, but that doesn't mean you can't enjoy them. Here's what the experts say. I think the fun of conspiracy theories is questioning everything, and knowing that we will never really know the truth.

Let's suppose for a moment that some conspiracy theory is true. What do you think it is? What if all our governments were actually controlled by aliens from another planet? Imagine it, governments run by aliens. It sounds bonkers, but wouldn't it be awesome? Okay, maybe not for you and me. But for them – those tip-top decision makers in charge of global relations - imagine the potential.

In truth, we are all ants waiting to meet our makers... or something like that. Our collaboration is a tool which will unify mankind. The one thing every single person has in common is that we are all going to die. We want to change that with our product which will make life easier, more productive and less stressful.

ACKNOWLEDGEMENT

Thank you to my previous colleagues who helped put this information together. We are so glad you enjoyed the book. Would you give it 5 stars for superior content and read level? If so, please share this information so others can find this hidden gem!

ABOUT THE AUTHOR

Jane Walters

Jane Walters is a former journalist, who has written both fiction and nonfiction books. She has written numerous articles for various publications such as "The Times", "New York Magazine"and "Newsday Weekly".